Simply for Kids!

Simply for Kids!

By Will Davis

authorHOUSE®

AuthorHouse™
1663 Liberty Drive
Bloomington, IN 47403
www.authorhouse.com
Phone: 1-800-839-8640

First published by AuthorHouse   12/01/2011

ISBN: 978-1-4634-3048-1 (sc)

Printed in the United States of America

CONTENTS

SPRING!

By Will Davis

The snow was melting!
The green grass was visible again!
Summer was coming,
But this was really spring.
It was warm again.
As we shed our heavy coats.
Mom and Dad, of course,
Would loudly object.
Because it was not warm enough.
The birds and the squirrels,
Had finally returned.
We knew this because of their chatter,
And beaughtiful, sweet songs
Could quite plainly, be heard.
It was time for those outdoor sports,
That we all loved so.
Baseball! Fishing! Biking! Hiking!
How we missed them so!
The trees with their buds,
Showing traces of green,
While the flowers prepared,
To dance with the wind,
Just like royal queens.
Dipping and bowing their heads,
In recognition of the coming of the green!
The boys and their young ladies,
Practicing, when they thought
No one could see,
What spring really meant for you and me,
As we embraced each other,
Very close and quite tightly!
While riding the roller coaster,
That some of us thought was true love!

SUMMER!

By Will Davis

School is out!
It's over with!
Summer vacation is here!
We have survived
The shut-up, pent-up
Desire to roam about free!
Digging up worms for fishing,
Maybe even teasing the girls,
So they would notice me!
What if the other guys
Were to catch me and see
ME kissing the girls in glee?
Going for bicycle rides,
With no place in mind.
Just cruising around
To see what wonders we could find.
Stopping at the old horse trough
For a drink of water or two.
Playing games of hide and seek,
About our small town.
The girls would join in our fun,
But we didn't mind.
The more kids there were,
The more fun we had,
During our vacation time!

AUTUMN

By Will Davis

I would wonder about the mystery of fall;
Why the leaves would change colors and all.
I was told by others that thought they knew.
The leaves had to fall to make room for those that are new.
When the weather grew cold, the leaves would fall.
But before they fell, they would change colors for all.
The green would change to red, yellow, gold, and brown.
Then they would let go of the tree and fall to the ground.
I would have to rake them up into piles.
It was hard work for a little one like me.
But then I would get to have some fun,
As I would get to jump into the pile joyfully!
My dad would come out with a stern look upon his face.
He would scold me quite heartily and put me in my place.
Then I would rake the leaves into piles again,
So me, my brother, and sisters could jump into the pile again.
Soon our fun and games were finally over.
Again we had to rake the leaves into a pile.
Dad would bring big bags out to put the leaves in.
Our fun was over, but in a few days we got to do it all over again!

WINTER!

By Will Davis

I remember, as a child,
How I wondered at
The snow drifting down,
Covering, with white
All that was around.
How, as children,
We couldn't wait
To go out and build a snowman
That looked like a clown.
The time we spent
Looking for just the right look;
The right size carrot for the nose,
The old scarf, from where? No one knows.
We did not have a top hat,
So we used an old bag
That was dirty and brown.
Set it upon his head for a crown.
Tree twigs for his arms.
Old gloves for hands, we found.
For his eyes, we used black coal.
For a mouth, an old, flattened tin can
That made him look quite stern.
Everything was just right.
Then would come our snowball fight.
Covered in snow, wet, cold, and shivering,
We would come inside, quivering.
A hot chocolate and wrapped in a warm blanket,
While we huddled next to the old warm, wood stove.
Drinking our hot chocolate
And listening to winter music.
And best of all, the Christmas carols,
To make us all happy and toasty warm,
Waiting for Santa Claus,
And the white Christmas to come!

SKIPPING SCHOOL!

By Will Davis

I remember one cold winter day,
My brother and I wanted to play.
So we decided, from school,
We would play hooky!
Everything went as planned.
We walked to school as usual,
But on the way, we made a detour.
Thinking that we would not be caught,
If we stayed away from the streets.
We wandered about the neighborhood,
Sneaking from one backyard to another,
Until we came upon the great river.
We followed the river for many long moments,
Watching the pieces if ice flow by,
Tumbling along in the bouncing current.
We threw snowballs at the ice,
Keeping score of the hits and misses.
We had no idea of the passage of time.
Soon, we decided it was time to go home.
We believed we had spent the entire day
Playing about the neighborhood and on the river.
Boy! Were we ever wrong about the passage of time!
To our dismay, when we got home, we discovered
That our day-long excursion was only two hours.
There was a great clamor when we entered the house.
We were quite cold from our adventure.
Our parents stared at us quite sternly.
Then they administered our punishment quite appropriately.
To bed we were sent, with our bottoms warmed quite nicely.
Here ends our tale of skipping school.
Don't do it, if you know what's good for you.
Because, if you're caught, your punishment will be the rule!

UGH!

By Will Davis

I went to the bathroom the other day.
Everything was fine and went my way.
The whole event went very well,
As all that was in—I did expel!
Unfortunately, for me, you see,
Good luck wasn't meant to be.
As everyone could tell by the smell,
For me, it did not really go that well.
It seems that in my great haste,
From my body to expel my waste,
I sat upon the seat and forgot one little item!
And with great ease, my pants, I did fill them!

THE LITTLE MOUSE!*

By Will Davis

I was up late this weekend day,
To the kitchen, I made my way.
Put the coffee pot to boil;
In the fry pan, I put some oil.
Put bread in the toaster to brown.
Still upon my face there was a frown.
Something didn't look quite right.
For right there in plain sight,
My coffee cup was standing upright.
I usually put it away upside down.
I must have forgotten, for I found
In a spot, that was unusual
There was a tiny black thread
Dangling from the top.
This was quite unusual.
Not sure just as to what it was,
I peeked inside, not disturbing the cup.
Inside, on the bottom, was a big black blob.
I did not touch it, for I knew
As soon as I saw it, I knew what to do.
I got a saucer from the cupboard above, and
Placed it on the top of that coffee mug.
Trapped inside, as safe as he could be,
Was this little mouse that came to visit me.
He was as cute as he could be.
Curled into a tight little ball,
Sleeping so soundly, and so peacefully.
I could do nothing, but let it be;
In spite of this compulsive revulsion, inside of me.
As I continued to prepare to feed me,
I knew as I ate, that it could not,
Should not, remain with me.
While that little mouse slept so soundly,
I pondered what must truly be.
Of course, for sure, he had to go!
I took him out to the back alley,
And with little ceremony, set him free!

THE MATTRESS TAG!.

By Will Davis

When I was just a snip of a lad,
I often wondered about mattress tags.
I asked my parents one day,
Why I should not take off that tag.
They showed me the printing upon it.
I read in my own little way,
"DO NOT REMOVE UNDER,
PENALTY OF THE LAW!"
"What does that mean?" I asked my paw.
He said quite jokingly,
"They will come and get you!
And take you very far away.
In a dark room with no windows,
They will definitely put you!
They'll feed you bread and water,
For the rest of your days.
You will have to wear the same clothes,
Day after day after day after day!
Forever and ever you will be,
Locked up and never set free!
You will never see Mommy and me,
Ever, never, and forever again!"
I was scared out of my wits,
And promised I would leave
That little white tag alone.
With that fear, he made me believe.
One day there was a great commotion.
At the front door, there was a lot of motion.
When through that door there came a huge package.
With two men in control,
Into the bedroom went the huge baggage.
I watched with curiosity,
And a great deal of wonder,
As the outer covering of that package
Was completely torn asunder.

When all had been removed completely,
There standing on its end,
Stood a spanking brand new mattress,
With fancy stitching end to end.
I marveled at the intricate design,
As the pattern swirled and intertwined.
I was surely hoping and praying,
That this new mattress would be mine.
Then I saw it! I could not turn away.
That little white tag
Looked as big as a bale of hay!
I could not help myself,
And took a hold of it.
I did not mean for it to be torn away!
I just wanted to see what it looked like.
Did not see as the men took the mattress away.
Instinctively, I grabbed that little white tag.
Because of curiosity, I wanted to see what it had to say!
When the mattress was moved away,
I instinctively tightened my grip,
Upon that teeny, tiny white tag.
Watched in horror as it was ripped away!
Just then, into the room stepped my dad.
"What's in your hand?" he asked sternly,
As I knelt on the floor with that damned tag!
"What did I tell you about that mattress tag?"
He addressed me in a voice that was very stern!
"Now you will have to go away!" he said,
"Until your lesson, you have learned!"
He had not forgotten from the other day, what he had said.
The evening meal went as expected.
I hardly ate a thing, as was expected.
Went to bed that night with the light on!
Lay awake for what seemed like an eon!
Then with a screaming and a wailing,
The lights went out with that eerie sound.
It was an air raid drill that I knew not of.
I screamed in terror as I dove under the bed.
Crawled to the furthest corner under the bed!
Trembled in terror as the sirens sounded.
When down the hallway I could hear,
The sound of heavy footsteps,

That, in me, put a great fear!
I scrunched myself into that corner as far as I could.
Listened as those heavy footfalls came near.
They were coming to get me, I was quite sure!
As those pounding feet came through the door!

EPITAPH TO THE MATTRESS TAG!

Parents shouldn't tell kids stories like that. Even as a joke. The foot steps I heard and feet, of course, belonged to my dad. He had come to see if I was okay. He had forgotten about the mattress tag. It was 1944-45 and practice air raids were quite common. I was a little kid and believed my dad about the Mattress tag. When the sirens sounded in the still of the night and all of the lights went out, the vision of storm troopers coming to take me away and put me into a dark room with no lights was made all to real when I heard my dad's footsteps coming down the dark hallway in the dark of the night. All I could see from under the bed in the dim glow of the flashlight he was carrying, was a pair of feet thumping on the hardwood floor coming in my direction!

Scared the hell out me! You better believe it!

I have never touched a mattress tag since!

MAD ELEPHANT!

By Will Davis

I looked at that elephant's
Beady, little fiery, red eye
And knew he was angry at me.
I ran like hell and didn't stop,
Until I was as far away as I could be.
I do not know what I had done,
That had made him quite so angry.
When I had finished my fearful run,
And sat upon the hard wet ground,
Gasping and breathing rather heavily,
I heard a familiar sound in the distance.
And when I looked up, I could see
That angry elephant was still after me!
I could not run any further,
And waited for him to come to me.
He stopped in front of me,
With both those mad-looking,
Beady little red eyes and,
Stared directly at me.
Reached out unexpectedly,
With his snake-like nose,
And wrapped it around my waist.
I truly thought it was the end of me.
Raised me up and curled his trunk;
Rolled me up unceremoniously.
Like a pretzel, and he carried me
Back to the circus grounds.
He was as tender as he could be,
With his gentle handling of me.
Carried me to the full to the brim water barrel,
And dumped me in head first to the waist,
And swished me around repeatedly.
Then he gently placed me upon the ground,
And walked away with tail and trunk,
Swinging to and fro quite happily.

PESKY CRITTERS!

By Will Davis

The Statue of Liberty stands so tall!
The symbol of freedom for us all.
It's such a shame it had to be done.
The pest control people had to come.
The caretaker called the exterminator, you see.
Invaded by pesky critters was the Statue of Liberty!
They were into every nook and cranny.
The food they nibbled on quite happily,
As they ran amuck all over this island,
That the U. S. government named Liberty!
The statue stood tall and straight,
While within the pesky vermin ate.
They chewed upon anything they could get.
They even chewed on those disgusting cigarettes!
The exterminators did their job.
At day's end, the statue was entirely free of that mob.
But, the very next day, it did not work so well,
Because those peaky, testy, swarming vermin
Came back to invade the statue again!
There was not much that could be done,
Because after all, those pesky critters
Were just very curious humans!

Isn't it nice to know that in this country you can poke fun at such a grand old monument as the Statue of Liberty without fear of retribution from our government?

LITTLE FLY ON THE WALL!

By Will Davis

Little fly on the wall,
How come it is
That you don't fall?
What is your secret?
Please do tell us all.
We won't hurt you,
At this particular time.
We are curious, you see,
As we write this rhyme.
Tell us your secret,
Please do.
We want to walk,
The walls like you!
To be able to go anywhere
At any time,
When it pleases us to do;
To walk the walls like you.
Don't fly away just yet.
Your secret we have to get.
So we can go and have fun,
Buzzing around the town,
Until we find
A place to set down.
To be able to upset that clown
Who turns frowns upside down.
To buzz about his head,
As he swats at us!
Until he kills us dead!

this little ditty took me just ten minutes to think up and write. It has no particular meaning. just a fun thing to do to pass the time this evening. enjoy it if you will, for it was writen in fun with no intended pun.

THE BIG TOP!
By Will Davis

As I and the other kids watched
The lions, tigers, panthers, and bears,
As they dutifully performed their acts,
In wonderful wide open-eyed stares.
Eating cotton candy and popcorn,
Eyeing the clowns whenever they drew near,
Wondering what foolish trick they would do next.
As the peels of laughter roared about us with the cheers.
Applauding the high wire acts performed without fear,
As the scantily clad men and women danced about merrily,
On those invisible wires strung up so high.
As the adults watched once more through a child's eyes,
The wondrous awe, as the acrobats flew up to the sky.
Cheering and applauding so loudly.
As each routine was perfectly executed.
Marveled that they performed so effortlessly!
As many of us wished we could fly so expertly.
Down to earth we came when the acts were completely done.
More clowns and playful animals did we see.
As the trained animals performed their acts so expertly.
Then all too soon, the show was finally done!
And we went home completely happy and satisfied that we had come.
Me and my brother were asleep in the back seat of the car.

OH, TO BE A BOY AGAIN!

By Will Davis

What better way to celebrate life,
Than to climb a tree up to the sky!
To be carefree and not worry about strife!
To enjoy our youth and not wonder why.

To be as a young lad,
Free of all the worlds of pain.
To roam about the forests and plains;
To drink it all in like a child again!

Running and playing with your best friend.
Hearing his excited yelps and barks of joy.
Running and chasing after the rubber ball,
As he plays with his master; the young boy.

Or digging for creepy, crawling things!
Hunting for worms and all kinds of bugs,
To use as bait when you go fishing.
Sometimes running home for your mother's hugs.

Maybe to join in with your friends,
In the many varied games you love to play.
Searching and finding various uckee things
To chase the girls with, while the games you play.

Riding your bicycle all around town,
Just to see the familiar sights and to hear the sounds.
Feeling the thrill of it all with the wind in your face,
As you take in all that you've seen many times a thousand.

When at day's end, you go home,
Where love and warm food await your enjoyment,
And you do your share of the family chores.
When completed, you lie on the parlor floor.

Listening to your parents while you watch T. V.
Occasionally bothered by your brother or your sister.
Once in a while, playing with the cat,
That for some reason, you named 'Mister

Bed time finally arrives and off you go,
So you can be assured of a good nights sleep.
Perhaps to dream of days to come.
Building memories you shall forever keep!

ODE TO THE MOUSE
or wait until I get you—you little sucker!

By W.C. Davis

I was sitting in my parlor one day
Sipping a brew and reading the paper,
When out of the corner of my eye,
A moving shadow I did spy.

I paid it no never mind.
As when I went to investigate,
To my dismay and chagrin,
My chair I did vacate.

There was nothing to see;
Nothing there for me to see.
Nonplused, I took my seat again.
Took up my paper to read again.

Thought nothing of it,
'Til I saw the shadow once again
Flitting across the floor with great speed,
Faster than the fittest of steeds.

There was naught for me to do,
But purchase a trap or two.
Setting them out strategically,
In hopes of getting one or two.

The first trap was a success.
One was trapped and removed.
Two days later, another succumbed.
Then to my great surprise,

There was a great big giant one!
Black with a big, fat, white belly!
I did not get to see his eyes,
For he was too quick for me to see!

As he scampered to and fro
Enjoying his newfound freedom,
I was perplexed that he remained free
For the traps he did avoid.

No matter the place or type of food,
He circled them with great ease.
Ran right over them as though they weren't there
And right across the top of my chair.

More traps I laid out for him.
To him, the fun was about to begin.
With great care and dexterity
He ate the cheese quite delicately.

Then scampered away in glee.
I could have sworn he was laughing at me!
More traps just wouldn't do.
There were enough, don't you see.

It would be just a matter of time
Before he would finally spend his time
Caught in one of those devices.
Squealing to be set free!

The next day at rest I was,
In my favorite easy chair.
Next to the bookcase you see,
When I reached out for a book to read.

Just as my hand touched the spine of the book,
Some instinct, at the bookcase, made me look.
There it sat, staring at me in all its proud little glory,
With what appeared to be a big wide grin, you see!

Just you wait and see! Ha! Ha! Ha!
Just you wait and see! Ha! Ha! Ha!
That dirty little fiend! That devil's apparition
Won't get the best of me! Ha! Ha! Ha!

I'm not quite sure, you see,
But I think he is getting the best of me!
I am not ready to give in.
I've just begun to fight, you see!

I cannot and will not let that
Little beast get the best of me.
I'm bigger than he is, and much smarter, too.
I am bound to see that creature caged in a zoo!

But when he sits and laughs at me,
That's more than I can stand to bear.
So the next time he shows, I must prepare,
To set the best of traps that there be.

I hope that when this is all done,
That he will be the only one.
Chasing mice is not my thing.
I'd rather be out dancing and dining.

It is not that I am being mean,
But that—and—little thing
Just doesn't belong in my abode.
So in the only way I know, he must be told!

He does not belong in this household!
A pet he shall not become.
His qualifications are not the best.
I'm searching for words to put this tale to rest.

A magic wand I could most assuredly use.
I know that I would put it to very good use.
I know my tale is quite not told.
For the mouse is much too much bold!

He still runs about free, you see.
Laughing at me, don't you see?
But his days are numbered for sure,
Because I'm about to shut his door!

This you must assuredly know,
There are no barriers for a mouse.
No matter the precautions,
He will find a way into your house!

In our most famous historic past,
The greatest of tales of mice abound.
The mouse has proven to be
The most durable mammal found!

From the fantastic Christmas stories
From yesterday and to those beyond.
There is no other more unwelcomed beast
To <u>not</u> be invited to the great family holiday feast!

Intelligent though it may well be,
This four-legged, creepy little creature,
Will become, as you all most definitely will see,
The big stupendous, and glorious main feature!

When upon that celebrated day,
He will become as no more.
When into my trap, he will stray,
To be as Poe's famous "NEVERMORE!"

I have planned extremely well.
With all of his smarts, he has learned
Of the many traps in his path, I have placed.
So I move them about with great care and concern.

In hopes that he will soon be captured.
Then all of my mouse problems
Will then be put to their final rest.
My home will then be rid of this pest!

As I retire upon Christmas Eve,
To dream of peace and the gifts,
I most definitely will happily receive.
A rustling and movement in the shadows is perceived!

I have come to a great realization,
That I am, quite honestly, to be a victim,
To that mouse's happy celebration,
Of that famous night in question.

Why did that creature have to pick on me!?
I was as happy in my home as I could be.
I know for sure, that Santa did not give him to me.
Where he came from is a great mystery.

I am hoping and praying to the powers that be,
That this small creature's visit to me,
Will be the end of it's short comings,
And the beginning of it's long goings for me.

The cheese I place upon the trap so delicately.
So my fingers do not get snapped so heavily.
He removes so carefully and stealthily.
To my great dismay to find the trap undisturbed and empty!

He has learned from my administrations,
To capture him with no quarter given,
To remove him from my presence,
He has proven to be very sneaky and unforgiving.

My tale has come to an unresolved end.
I will continue to stalk and trail him.
To ply him with all of the goodies that I can,
Until he is captured and put away for good!

You know, don't you, that this is not really the end.
That this mouse just, quite possibly, might win in the end.
And follow me to the grave, when at life's end,
To our respective resting places we shall end.

I know that I will eventually have to go,
When to my grave I will descend.
Know this for sure, and with great certainty,
That little beast will most assuredly go before me!

THE CIRCUS!
(Through the eyes of a ten-year-old boy)

By Will Davis

I went to the circus the other day.
I got to see all of the clowns do their thing.
But most of all—the most important thing
Was I got to see all of the animals at play!
I got to eat popcorn, peanuts, and cotton candy,
Hamburgers, hot dogs, and many other things!
But the strangest of all was I got to eat
These great big elephant ears!
The money I spent filled my daddy's eyes with tears!
Before we went home and called it a day.
When all of the shows were completed and done,
We got to visit all of the animals, one by one.
The biggest of all were those huge, gray, behemoths!
With short, rope-like tails and their long serpentine noses,
They were great things of wonder to see.
I paid no mind to the warnings issued to me.
I was under the wrong end you see!
And that great big behemoth of an elephant,
Quite unceremoniously proceeded to poop all over me!

Based upon a true event!

HOT DOGS!.

By Will Davis

I was preparing hot dogs
For a meal the other day.
When a very young friend
Happened to come my way.

He watched with great interest,
As my meal I prepared to eat.
I put the dogs in some buns,
And he said how that looked so neat.

I began to apply the condiments.
Then into the bun, that dog went.
When I applied the yellow mustard,
He said, "That looks just like my puppy's POOP!"

When he had gone on his way,
I looked at that hot dog in a bun,
And came to the realization,
That, that little boy had spoiled my fun in a bun!

Composed 8-26-2008 at 2:00 p.m., while cooking hot dogs for a snack!

ABOUT THE AUTHOR

This is my first attempt at getting published nationally. From my days in high school, and as far back as I can remember in grade school, I liked to write. I began writing my poetry to impress a girl younger than I of my romantic intentions. Bear in mind, I was a high school kid at that time. I continued to write many more poems about all subjects down through the years. Unfortunately, during my hitch in the Air Force, more than two hundred poems that I had written and kept in the bottom of my bedroom closet were lost! My dad, in the process of spring cleaning, had found my box of poetry written upon many scraps of paper. He didn't think they were of any value and tossed them into the garbage, along with my comic book collection (which I think he gave to a relative). Fortunately, at least fifty to sixty were saved, and I continued to add to them over the years in my spare time. To date, I have written close to 200 poems, which I hope to have published. Enclosed is a selection of poems written with kids in mind. Many of these were written after I retired, and were based upon true events or ideas I had gotten from out of nowhere. The one titled, "HOT DOG!" and "THE LITTLE MOUSE!" was written just a few weeks ago.

Here, then, are my poetic endeavors, which I hope will be received enthusiastically.

Printed in the United States
By Bookmasters